Originally published in 1995 by Allan T Condie Publications.

This edition published in 2010 by Japonica Press
Low Green Farm, Hutton, Driffield, East Yorkshire, YO25 9PX.

ISBN: 978-1-904686-18-7

A catalogue record for this book is available from the British Library

Printed and bound in the UK by JF Print Ltd., Sparkford, Somerset.

Original design, layout and editing by Allan T Condie.

INTRODUCTION

In a changing world it is heartening to be able to tell the story of the later period of the development of Massey-Ferguson tractors.

Whilst this book was originally envisaged as one which would cover the period from 1965 onwards, due to the importance which the post 1958 models have in telling the whole story of the 100, 200 and 500 series, the opportunity has been taken to preface the main part of this book with a resume of developments once the TE20 had been updated.

In dealing with tractors in the post 1965 period, the complexities of model designations and the increasing capability of plants to build tractors to exact customer specifications makes the job of giving a complete picture of any range almost impossible. This book does, however, give an overview of models produced from 1958 to 1980 and slightly later in some cases.

Carlton, September 1995...   **Allan T. Condie**

ACKNOWLEDGEMENTS

The author would like to thank the following for their assistance with information and illustrations for this book. David Bate, the late Charles Cawood, Bob Moorhouse, Stephen Moate, Mervyn Spokes Darren Tebbitt and Massey-Ferguson.

Massey Ferguson Tractors from 1958

To fully understand the evolution of the MF range of tractors once the 'two line' policy of maintaining both Massey Harris and Ferguson models was discontinued in 1958 we need to return to 1946 and the evolution of the Ford Ferguson 9N into the Famous Fergie 20.

The Fergie 20 incorporated all the desirable features which Harry Ferguson had envisaged his 'Ferguson System' should offer. Hydraulic three point linkage with draft control, a central PTO, safe starting by means of the gearshift, adjustable wheel track with beam type front axle, and an overhead valve petrol engine.

Market forces decided that over the next 10 years the TE-20 appeared in many variations. The full story of that tractor and its antecedents is covered in our companion volume "Vintage Tractor Special - 1, The Fergie 20 Family. Low cost fuel and finally diesel variations appeared, with tractors also being built in lesser numbers at the Detroit plant of Harry Ferguson Ltd. The Banner Lane plant at its inception in 1946 was one of the most modern automobile production plants in the world, capable of producing in excess of 300 units a day. It was owned by the Standard Motor Co. Ltd., who built the tractors on behalf of Harry Ferguson Ltd., and also supplied their own engines, which were of a type also used in their 'Vanguard' range of cars and vans. As the engines were not available when production began, American Continental units were imported, and these continued to be used in US production until the 1960s.

Whilst the TE20 remained the only model built in the UK until 1958, the US variants evolved from the TO20, through the TO30 with a larger engine, to result in the introduction of the TO35 in 1954. Whilst this model retained all the essential features of the '20' it incorporated a dual range gearbox, larger engine, and hydraulics which also gave position control as well as the familiar Ferguson patented draft control system, provided for by a hydraulic pump of an increased capacity. It is worth pointing out that even today the Scotch yoke piston type of hydraulic pump is used in most MF tractors.

The smaller scale of production meant that the new model could be handled at Detroit with little disruption to production. However, one event which was to shape the future of Ferguson tractors was the acquisition of Ferguson by Massey Harris in 1954, which was publicly called a 'merger'.

The then current range of Massey Harris tractors were not enjoying record sales, and the

TO35 was taken and revamped as a true 'Rowcrop' tractor with normal wide beam front axle, or the option of single or vee twin front wheels. This tractor was first marketed through the Massey Harris dealers in America as the Massey Harris 50, and its development had a bearing on later US and UK built models as we shall see. The Ferguson dealers protested, and the result was the Ferguson 40. The only real differences were in sheet metal work and paint finish. Both these tractors featured Continental engines.

In the United Kingdom, the move towards Compression Ignition engines in the majority of tractors was well under way by the mid 1950s, and Ferguson had made use of the 23C Standard engine in the 35. Some of these units were exported and fitted in TO35 tractors at the Detroit plant. The end of the two line policy also coincided with the conclusion of negotiations to give Massey Ferguson ownership of the Banner Lane plant at Coventry, and also saw the acquisition of Frank Perkins Ltd., of Peterborough, the diesel engine builder, and these two events were to have far reaching consequences for the future of Massey Ferguson Tractors.

Whilst spark ignition engines were still sourced from Standard in the UK, and Continental in the USA, the MF range were now to become available with Perkins diesels. Massey Harris models were discontinued and the only former Massey model to be retained was the Massey Ferguson 50, which acquired revised tinwork and the option of the Perkins A3.152 diesel engine. This engine was also fitted to the MF35.

The availability of a suitable Perkins engine in the 50HP class enabled Massey Ferguson to launch the 65 in 1958. This tractor utilised the same transmission line as the 35 and 50 models, but reduction hubs were added to the rear axle shafts to absorb some of the increased torque from the Perkins 4.192 four cylinder diesel engine. The Ferguson 40 tinwork was used on UK assembled units, having been made redundant at the end of the two line policy, whilst the 65 Dieselmatic sold in the USA and Canada had the same styling as the MF50, and the 65 was also available with a Continental Petrol engine. All three basic models, the 35, 50 and 65 received enhanced specifications in due course, with Multi-Power, and more powerful diesel engines, with direct injection.

The scene was now set to provide the basis for the next generation of tractors, apart from the fact that the French MF plant, inherited through Massey Harris, launched their own small tractor in 1963. The 25, this tractor had been developed using a four cylinder Perkins 4.99 engine in a Fergie 20, the final model receiving the slightly larger 4.107 engine. This tractor was also known as the 30 and the 825 during its short production run. One unusual feature of this model was the location of the hydraulic pump in the top housing of the transmission.

New Designs for the Sixties - the 100 Series.

By the early sixties, it can now be seen that there was a certain amount of standardisation in the MF tractors built in both Eastern and Western Hemispheres, unlike Fords, for example, whose designs in England and the USA were totally different.

With the trend towards unified product lines moving ahead in all automotive fields, MF took the step to introduce a completely new range of models in 1965, with unified styling and specifications worldwide. The demand for Gasoline engines was still evident in the USA, and thus Continental engines still appeared in these tractors.

The MF135 replaced the 35, the MF150 the MF50 (available only in the Western hemisphere), and the 165 the 65. In fact these models bore a similar relationship to each other as the 35-50-65 did. The use of Perkins engines saw the MF135 and MF150 fitted with the AD3.152 engine, the MF165 had the AD4.203 of its predecessor. Whilst Continental engines were still available in all these models, the Z134 in the 135 Special, the Z145 in the MF135 deluxe, and MF150, and the G176 in the MF165, Petrol versions of the Perkins engines were developed and the later MF135/MF150 became available with the Perkins AG3.152 engine and the 165 with the AG4.212. Six forward speeds were provided in all models along with two reverse, but the equipping of any model with "Multipower" doubled those. The 135 retained the beam type front axle of its predecessor, whilst the other models had the usual arrangement to allow the use of row crop type equipment. All models had a new styling with "squared up" appearance.

The 175 was a new model, and featured a Perkins 4.236 engine. This was designed specially to fit the tractor, and was the first Perkins engine to feature the inlet and exhaust manifolds on the same side. Indeed, when the 165 was updated in 1968, the old style AD4.203 engine had given way to a new unit based on the 4.236 but with shorter stroke, the 4.212. The American built 180 was similar but designed for rowcrop work.

Hydraulics on all models except the 130 were improved, with the addition of 'pressure control' which allowed draft control to be used with trailing implements. One feature of all models

apart from the 130 was the use of many common transmission components.

In 1971 the 175 was replaced by the 178 with a larger engine, the Perkins A4.248.

In November 1971, in time for the Smithfield Show, the 100 series was expanded to cover six models. These consisted of the three models of the basic range, which could be purchased in 'Standard Rig', with no Multipower, manual steering, live PTO, etc. often to suit export markets. The 135 and 165 continued as before, whilst the 178 had been replaced by the 185 earlier in the same year. The basic range were very price competitive for those customers who did not want too much sophistication. The above did not feature gearbox spacers.

The first cabs made available for the 100 series were not safety cabs, indeed they were constructed of fibreglass. The first safety cabs were of composite construction with canvas (plastic) infill, and the option of engine side shrouds which diverted engine heat to warm the cab. From 1971 the option of a rigid clad type cab was available at extra cost. In due course full safety cabs to 'Q' specification had to be supplied for UK use, but as the 100 series were being produced mainly for overseas markets by the mid seventies, it was often the case that domestic sales received proprietary cabs.

One of the problems when a cab was fitted was the restricted access to the driving position. This was overcome by introducing a spacer on the 100 series 'Super Spec' tractors from late 1971, which fitted between the gearbox and rear axle and lengthened the wheelbase of the tractor. This allowed the fitting of a more spacious safety cab. It also altered the weight distribution of the tractor to advantage, allowing the attachment and use of heavier implements without the need for front weights. With these improvements, including the use of spacers, the 135 became the 148, the 165 became the 168, the 135 the 148, and a stretched version of the 185, the 188 was also introduced, in time for Smithfield Show in 1971, where the improved range were shown. The 'Super- Spec' tractors also had independent PTO, Multipower transmission, spring suspension seat, high capacity hydraulic pump, and in the case of the 188 only, power steering and power adjusted wheel track.

In practice the range of models was complicated by the fact that if a customer desired he could up-grade a basic model or down grade a 'Super-spec' model. Where Multi- Power was not specified a new eight speed gearbox was offered on all models except the 135 and 165 which still used a six speed unit.

But the spacer idea was also put to good use in using the space for an optional 'creeper' gearbox in place of the spacer. As far as normal gearboxes were concerned, the 130 had an eight speed gearbox within high and low ratios, whilst the other models had a basic six speed transmission over high and low ratios, which became 12 with the application of 'Multipower', which was optional.

The smallest model sold in the UK was the 130, which was an update of the MF30 built in France, with a Perkins 4.107 four cylinder diesel. On the other hand, the largest conventional tractor available on world markets was the US built 1100, fitted with the Perkins A6.354 diesel or a Waukesha F320-G six cylinder petrol engine. This became the 1130 when fitted with a turbocharged version of the diesel engine, the Perkins AT6.354. The 1080 was a relative, but this had a Perkins 4.318 diesel; this tractor was derived from the US built 180 and was also assembled in France. The ultimate in 100 series power was the 1150 built at the Detroit plant from 1970-72, which featured a Perkins V8.510 diesel. At the other end of the scale, the French plant specialised in the Vineyard (Vigneron) and Orchard (Etroit) models based on the 130 and 135 tractors. By using derated and uprated engines 122, 140 and 145 models were offered, the 122 Vigneron having a 4.99 rather than the 4.107 engine of the 130, and the 140 and 145 engines used the 3.152 engine set to run at 2150 rpm and 2250 rpm respectively rather than the standard 2000 rpm.

Four Wheel Drive Interlude

This new development from Massey Ferguson was launched in December 1971 and the tractor bore no real relationship to any previous model. It had 4 equal size wheels and employed centre pivot steering. The tractor was equipped with the Perkins A6.354 diesel engine rated at 105HP. Ferguson system hydraulics with draft control were standard, as was an isolated quiet cab in anticipation of forthcoming legislation. The model remained in production until 1980. Its replacement, the 1250, appeared in 1979 with the Perkins A6.3544 112HP engine and lasted until 1982.

The 500 Series

Further legislation with regard to cabs was to have far reaching effects on tractor design in the 1970s. From the 1st September 1977 it became a legal requirement for all tractors supplied new in the United Kingdom to have a cab fitted which when all windows were closed did not allow noise levels of over 90db inside. Massey Ferguson responded with the creation of a totally new range of tractors to encompass this requirement, placing a special emphasis on driver comfort. Whilst some manufacturers chose to upgrade current models and so maintain location and mounting of all controls on the tractor transmission and body, the new MF 500 range utilised remote linkages so that all controls were mounted

on the cab structure apart from the gear levers. This allowed a flat floor cab to be adopted and further advances were made in the provision of a heating and ventilation system comparable with that fitted to other motor vehicles.

In addition to the new cab features, the 500 range incorporated improved hydraulics, and PTO drive arrangements. The four original models in the range, the 550, 565, 575 and 590 utilised many common transmission and hydraulic components; the basic drive-line having been inherited from the previous range. The engines fitted are tabulated below along with the models they nominally replaced.

- 550 with Perkins A3.152s engine developing 47HP replaced the 148

- 565 with Perkins A4.236 engine developing 60HP replaced the 165

- 575 with Perkins A4.236 engine developing 66HP replaced the 168

- 590 with Perkins A4.248 engine developing 75HP replaced the 185/8

It is interesting to note that the Perkins A4.212 used in the 165 was discarded in favour of a derated A4.236 engine.

The fifth model in the range the 595, has a more complex history. The 1080 which was built from 1967 on was replaced by a new model the 595 MkI in 1974. To understand the complexities of the larger models manufactured by MF at the time, we must look to the models produced at the Canadian plant from 1972 particularily for the North American market, the 1105 and 1135 which both featured the Perkins A6.354T engine and the 1155 which utilised the Perkins V8.540 engine. These restyled models were joined in 1973 by the 1085 which was, in effect an upgraded 1080. This was sold in modified form in the UK as the 595, and also as the 285 in overseas territories without the cab. From 1978 the 575 and 590 became available in 4WD. The 595 which had become the 595 MkII by virtue of a minor restyle in 1976, was also available with 4WD.

The 500 series continued in production until early 1982. In their original form they were rather unpopular with customers due to the single door configuration of the cab. In mid 1979 2 door cabs were introduced and from mid 1980 the cabs were painted red right up to roof level. Some models appeared in the Spring of 1981 with a new grille with integral headlamps.

The 200 Series

The 285 introduces us to the 200 series which was launched in the UK in 1979. These replaced the entire 100 series and had their roots in the

1975 range of smaller tractors launched in the Western Hemisphere. The 1979 range consisted of 5 basic models as follows:-

- 240 with Perkins AD3.152 engine developing 34HP replaced the 135.

- 250 with Perkins AD3.152 engine developing 40IIP.

- 270 with Perkins AD4.236 engine developing 55HP.

- 290 with Perkins AD4.248 engine developing 65HP.

- 298 with Perkins AD4.318.2 engine developing 78HP.

The 240 and 250 were available with 8 speed manual transmission only, plus power assisted steering. Only the 240 had mechanically actuated drum brakes. The other three models offered 12 Speed Multi-Power as an alternative, and along with the 250 featured hydraulically actuated immersed disk brakes. The Hydraulics featured quadramatic draft and position control. Auxiliary hydraulics were optional on the 250 and standard on the 270, 290 and 298.

For sale in the UK, the 240, when introduced to the UK market in 1979, featured a quick detach cab. Also introduced at the same time was the 265, a utility alternative to the 565 again with 565 running gear for the UK livestock market where a lift-off cab was required. The 200 range in the Western Hemisphere had been launched in 1975 and the 230, 245, 255, 265, 275 and 285 were the result, it is to be noted that different model numbers were used for different territories, the complete range first sold in America were as follows.

- 230 with Perkins AD3.152 engine developing 34HP.

Or with Continental Z145 4 cylinder gasoline engine.

- 245 with Perkins AD3.152 engine developing 42HP.

Or with Continental Z145 4 cylinder gasoline engine.

- 255 with Perkins AD4.236 engine developing 52HP.

- 265 with Perkins AD4.236 engine developing 60HP.

- 275 with Perkins AD4.248 engine developing 67HP.

- 285 with Perkins AD4.318 engine developing 78HP.

Later 200 series tractors with spark ignition engines received Perkins units equivalent to the diesel models.

As we approach the cut-off date for this publication, it only remains to cover the 2000 series launched in 1979. This range which covered the important 100-130HP bracket and consisted of 2 models, the 2640 coming in the Spring and the 2680 in the Autumn.

- 2640 with Perkins A6.354.4 engine developing 104HP.

- 2680 with Perkins AT6.354.4 engine developing 120HP.

Connections

The Italian firm of **Landini** had roots back into the nineteenth century and produced its first tractors in the 1920s. Single cylinder designs with surface ignition engines were prevalent until 1957 when an agreement was reached with Perkins diesels to build these under licence and install them in a new range of tractors. Following the acquisition of Perkins by MF in 1959, Landini was acquired by them in 1960. During the period covered by this book Landini tractors continued to be built to their own distinctive designs, but certain crawler models were sold in MF colours. Landini also supplied 4WD front axles to other MF factories, and in due course certain MF models began to be assembled at the Landini factory.

IMT, or to give the concern its full title of Industrija Masina Traktora of Beograd, Yugoslavia started building tractors in the late 1940s. Ferguson designs were adopted and built under licence until 1968 when the agreement expired. From that date, models have generally followed MF designs and the use of Perkins engines has continued. The IMT 539 could be easily identified as being the old MF35 but larger models were also produced which had some allegiance to the 100 series.

EBRO in Spain was originally allied to the Ford Motor Co., but the Franco government nationalised the concern in 1954. In the 1960s the Fordson Super Major was built using the tooling formerly used at the Dagenham plant in England. Then in 1966 agreement was reached with Massey Ferguson and Perkins to build MF tractors. Some strange things happened however, such as the introduction of some 'bastard' models starting with the EBRO 155, which featured MF 100 series tinwork but underneath was really a Spanish built Fordson Super Major. Once EBRO managed to set its sights on selling tractors abroad, the 100 series tinwork was altered to disguise the MF 'look' and the 155 became the 160E. By fitting Perkins engines the 470 and 684E models were created.

In addition, some MF 100 series tractors were sold in Spain painted Blue & Silver and badged as EBROs.

The Ford-Ferguson 9N was the tractor which laid the foundations in design for all subsequent Ferguson System tractors. Harry Ferguson would have like the tractor to have been equipped with an overhead valve engine, but in order to get production rolling a side valve unit which was in effect half a Mercury V8 was used.

The original Fergie 20 is seen here with a two furrow plough   The Continental Z-120 engines had to be specially imported and import licenses obtained; the use of a UK built engine as soon as available became a priority.

Above: The TED-20 was the popular Ferguson tractor of the early 1950s and embodied all the improvements possible once the Standard Motor Co. began building TE-20 tractors for Harry Ferguson Ltd. at Banner Lane, Coventry in 1946. The low-cost fuel model was a later addition to the range, featuring a Standard overhead valve engine.

Left: Limited production of Ferguson TO-20 tractors was achieved in the USA from October 1948. The tractor was upgraded in August 1951 as the TO-30 and the model shown here, the TO-35 was produced from 1954. This introduced the dual range gearbox and draft control/position control to the Ferguson range. Continental engines were used throughout. The Ferguson TO-35 featured a green and beige paint scheme to make it look different from the equivalent Ford models which were red and beige.

Below: It was to be nearly another two years before the FE-35 appeared in the United Kingdom and the Coventry built tractors featured different styling. A TVO engined example is seen here, the Standard built engine now having an 87mm bore.

Opposite page top: The Standard 23C diesel was also offered in the FE-35, which was finished in a grey and gold colour scheme.

Opposite page Centre & Bottom: The MF-35 tractors built at the Detroit plant retained the TE-20 style of grille even after the Massey Harris - Ferguson merger. The paint finish was red and metallic grey from 1959 and from the same year Perkins Diesels were available. We see here a Deluxe specification tractor with 'Power Shift' rear wheels, extra fuel capacity, and oversize tyres.

Opposite page top: The MF35 featured the Perkins P3.152 engine from November 1959. This followed the fitment of a P3(TA) engine and also a Fordson 'Dexta' type F3 engine to prototypes in 1958. The engine is shown in the two views in the centre of the page.

Opposite page bottom: The 35X featured a more powerful version of the Perkins 3-152 engine, the A3-152, and was produced from 1962. Although production of the 35 ceased in the UK in 1964, assembly continued elsewhere - the tractor shown above on this page was assembled in France.

Right: Ferguson tractors were always popular with industrial and public works users. Here is the 35X, finished in yellow livery and with industrial type mudguards. Other options were alternative tyre sizes, hydraulic brakes, and choice of standard fenders.

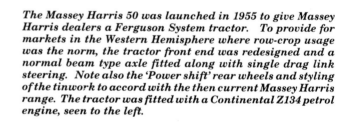

The Massey Harris 50 was launched in 1955 to give Massey Harris dealers a Ferguson System tractor. To provide for markets in the Western Hemisphere where row-crop usage was the norm, the tractor front end was redesigned and a normal beam type axle fitted along with single drag link steering. Note also the 'Power shift' rear wheels and styling of the tinwork to accord with the then current Massey Harris range. The tractor was fitted with a Continental Z134 petrol engine, seen to the left.

When M-H-F launched the 50, Ferguson dealers protested, and the result was the Ferguson 40 which was only produced for two years from 1956-1957. It only differed from the M-H 50 in tinwork and paint finish, the Ferguson version being painted beige and green. The top illustration shows a tractor to standard specification, whilst to the left is a high clearance model, and below the other options of a single or vee twin front wheels. The wheel options were also available on the Massey Harris 50.

The MF 65 was the Massey Ferguson response to the need for a tractor in the 50HP class to compete with Ford and Nuffield. Following the realisation that the LTX prototypes would cost too much to put into production, the Western Hemisphere practice of modifying the existing model to suit was adopted. The 35 transmission was taken, and given epicyclic final reduction gearing on the outer ends of the rear axle shafts, and a Perkins 4.192 diesel was fitted. Front axle and front end were pure Ferguson 40/ Massey Harris 50, and to save on costs the press tools for the 40 tinwork, (now out of production) were shipped to the UK and the 65 given its distinctive styling. The final reduction gearing was to compensate for increase in wheel size and increased engine power; the existing gearbox being able to absorb the increased torque at higher speeds. Disc brakes were fitted, and the abandonment of the Ferguson style front axle, as inherited from its precursor, the MH50, allowed for the fitting of a single front wheel or vee twin wheels where necessary.

Above: *Also available were the 65R and 65S industrial models. Whilst the 65S had a normal dual clutch transmission, the 65R had an 11.75" Borg & Beck Torque Convertor and a shuttle transmission which gave four speeds in each direction. A diff. lock and handbrake were optional, as was a crankshaft hydraulic pump to operate loading shovels, etc.   Power assisted steering was also available.*

Below: The MF65 Dieselmatic shown in the bottom illustration as sold in the Western Hemisphere retained the 'Massey Harris' look too, however for sale in the USA a petrol engined version using the Continental G.176 engine seen to the right.

With the end of the two line policy, the Ferguson 40 and
Massey Harris 50 were replaced by one model, the MF-
50, seen above and below. Whilst the tractor in the top
picture has the Continental Z134 engine shown on the
right, the MF50 was also available with the Perkins
3.152 diesel from 1959 onwards as seen below.

Above: The M-F Super 90 was only sold in the Western Hemisphere. This featured either a Continental E242 Gasoline engine or the Perkins A4-300 unit seen below. This was the first engine developed specially for tractor use by Perkins following the M-F takeover. An eight or sixteen speed shift-on-the-go transmission was employed and this model replaced the 85 which had been produced in 1958. This tractors design was to influence later models in the above 60HP power class.

Above: A Fergie 20 was fitted with a Perkins 4.99 engine as the development tractor for the French built M-F 30 seen here. This little tractor used the uprated version of the 4.99, the 4.107. Its intention was to provide a small tractor for the French market, where many small farmers still used motor cultivators. It was updated and restyled to fit into the 100 range in 1965 as the 130. The example below and in the upper illustration on the opposite page is one for UK sale.

Below: For export to the Western Hemisphere and other territories the 130 was available without lights as seen here.

Above: **The four models in the 100 range as originally available in the United Kingdom.**

Below: **The 135 replaced the popular 35X and the example shown here features Multi-Power which increased the available gear ratios.**

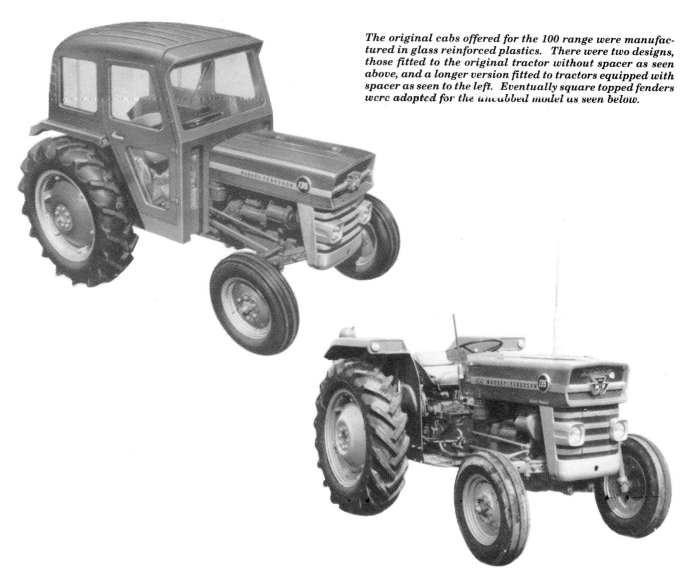

The original cabs offered for the 100 range were manufactured in glass reinforced plastics. There were two designs, those fitted to the original tractor without spacer as seen above, and a longer version fitted to tractors equipped with spacer as seen to the left. Eventually square topped fenders were adopted for the uncabbed model as seen below.

The illustrations on this page show MF135s as sold in the Western Hemisphere, in particular the range offered in Canada from 1965. The vineyard model is seen from the rear (right) whilst below is the Orchard model, but fitted with a Perkins A3.152 diesel. It was also available with a Perkins AG3.152 Gasoline engine. This model was only 49" to the top of the steering wheel, and featured an 8 speed manual transmission.

All 135 models sold in the USA and Canada had outboard headlamps.

Right: The 135 Special also featured the Perkins AG3.152 gasoline engine with a six speed transmission.

Left: The 135 Standard offered the choice of the usual Perkins A3.152 diesel or AG3.152 gasoline engines and the option of 8 speed or 12 speed Multi-Power transmissions.

Right: For comparison, the 135 for the Eastern Hemisphere is seen with lights recessed, and vertical exhausts were preferred.

Left and Below: Late 135s had a revised front axle design and an improved engine with new type injection pump.

Left: The 135S was developed for industrial applications, and could be finished in an alternative yellow and grey colour scheme. The example here is fitted with a spacer to lengthen the wheelbase.

Opposite page: Whilst petrol (gasoline) engined 135 tractors in the Western Hemisphere used Continental and later Perkins engines there were some built in the UK with Standard 87mm petrol engines taken from stock. These were kept as demonstrators and lent out to Show Jumping events and the like where the quieter running of the petrol engines did not disturb the horses.

Left: MF Vineyard tractors were built at the French plant and the MF135 vineyard model is seen here. This tractor had a 39" minimum track width. A 135 Orchard was also available with a 54" track width. The model was also offered with an uprated engine as the 140.

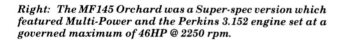

Right: The MF145 Orchard was a Super-spec version which featured Multi-Power and the Perkins 3.152 engine set at a governed maximum of 46HP @ 2250 rpm.

Left: Vineyard versions of the MF130 were also offered. The 122 seen here featured the Perkins 4.99 engine and was rated at 24HP. The 130 Vineyard used the slightly larger 4.107 engine and the 130 was also available as an orchard model.

Right: The Perkins A3.152 engine as fitted to many MF135 tractors. The standard unit gave 37.88HP @ 2000 rpm.

Above and Below. The 135 with Standard 87mm Petrol engine.

Above: The 150 was a model not sold in the UK - it was if you want to put it succinctly a cross between the 135 and 165, and successor to the MF50. The high clearance version with Continental Gasoline engine is seen here.

Left: A Perkins AG3.144 petrol engined 150 in standard wheel configuration.

Bottom: Another Continental engined tractor, this time in Vee twin front wheeled rowcrop guise.

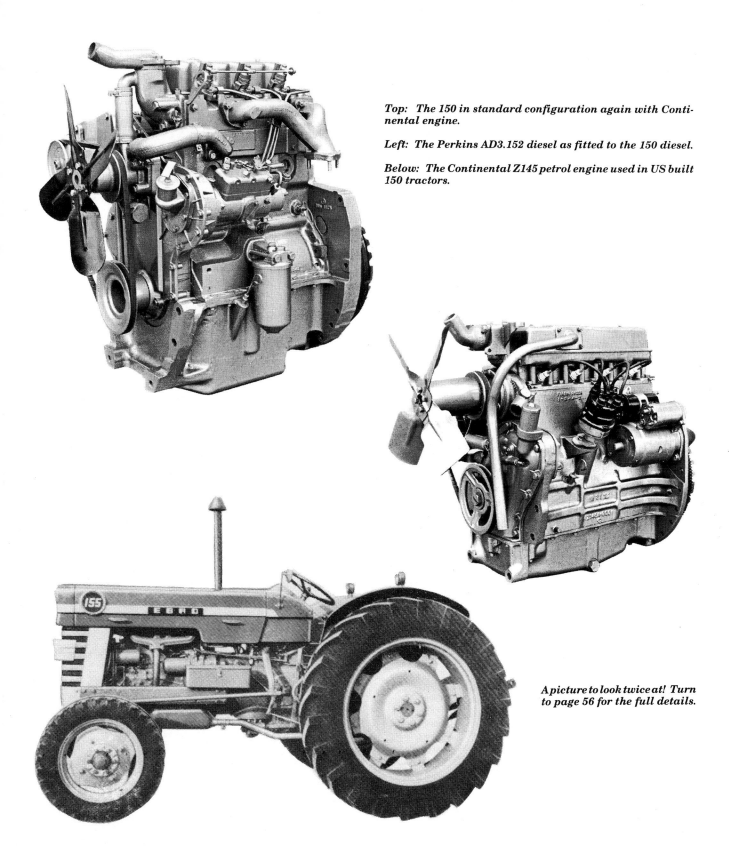

Top: The 150 in standard configuration again with Continental engine.

Left: The Perkins AD3.152 diesel as fitted to the 150 diesel.

Below: The Continental Z145 petrol engine used in US built 150 tractors.

A picture to look twice at! Turn to page 56 for the full details.

Left: The original 165 featured a Perkins AD4.203 engine inherited from the 65 and could be easily identified by the exhaust on the left side of the tractor. This example is a Coventry built one.

Above: An early Detroit built 165 showing the different lighting arrangements for the USA. Also of interest is the mid-mounted mower.

Right: Front weights were becoming a necessary accessory by the 1960s with the increased weight of rear mounted implements and MF provided easily attached units which were fitted to a bar on the front casting of the tractor.

Right: The original AD3.152 Perkins engine fitted to the 165.

Above and right: The 165 was produced from 1965-68 when it was also available in 'Super Spec' form as the 168. Later tractors as seen here featured the new Perkins AD4.212 engine as seen here, with the exhaust on the right side.

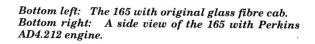

Bottom left: The 165 with original glass fibre cab.
Bottom right: A side view of the 165 with Perkins AD4.212 engine.

Above: Two views of the Perkins AD4.212 engine fitted to later MF165 tractors.

Opposite page: The 165 was probably the most popular of the 100 series MF tractors sold in the United Kingdom and these two working shots show the kind of work which the tractor was best suited to.

Below: The 168 was one of the 'Super-Spec' tractors added to the range in 1971. The extra features such as the spring suspension seat and the gearbox spacer are clearly seen.

Left: The 175 was the largest offering for UK consumption. The Perkins 4.236 engine gave 63HP. This is an early example with cast front wheel centres. Note the power adjusted variable track rear wheels, a feature which was not to prove over popular in the UK.

Above and left: The Italian Selene SAS concern produced this equal wheeled 4WD version of the 175. Little else is known about this adaptation as we acquired the photographs with no accompanying information.

Left: Later 175 tractors dispensed with the cast front wheel centres and had wheel weights inside the front pressings instead. Rear wheels have also given way to standard pressings.

Right: Another view of the later 175; an easy identification feature is the location of the steering drag link, which on early tractors was in a higher position.

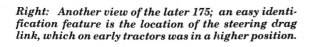

Left: The Perkins AD4.236 engine as fitted to the MF175.

Above and below: The 175 became the 178 after 1968 and was fitted with the Perkins AD4.248 engine which was a bored out AD4.236.

Left: The MF178 with PAVT rear wheels and cast fronts.
Below: The 178 with original design of MF glass fibre cab.

Left: Not quite what it seems. Whilst badged as a 178, this is in fact the 188 which featured a gearbox spacer. Whilst the 185 nominally replaced the 178 in 1971, 178 tractors were still being built until 1972. This illustration is of one of the prototypes.

Above and below: The 180 was designed expressly for the North American market and although available in conventional four wheeled form, it was most popular in the configuration seen here with vee twin front wheels. Note also the flat floor to the operators area which, with an adjustable steering column, allowed the operator to stand up or sit down.

Above: The 180 was offered with the option of a Continental G206 Gasoline engine. Even in 1965 spark ignition engines were still popular in the USA and Canada due to the low tax on gasoline. It was built from 1965 to 1974.

Right: The diesel 180 used the Perkins AD4.236 engine. Note however that with this model the engine did not totally support the front end of the tractor; subframes between the clutch housing and the front end were provided.

Below: The British built 188 was the 'Super-spec' version of the 185 and offered, from 1971, gearbox spacer, PAVT rear wheels, and spring suspension seat.

Above: The first generation of safety cabs offered for the MF100 range for the UK market were steel framed with flexible cladding Seen here are cabs on the 135, 165, 178 and 1080 models (qv.), the last model being the only one to feature steel cladding throughout. The heating system collected waste heat from the engine by means of the plastic side screens and diverted it into the cab.

Below: Another view of 135, 178 and 165 tractors with cabs. All tractors sold in the UK after 1st September 1970 were required to have factory fitted safety cabs.

Left: A 178 with MF loader loads a tipping trailer.

Right: Selene SAS offered this 4WD conversion for the 165 and 175 tractors.

Above: The 1080 was assembled in the France and was introduced in 1969, with safety cab, in the UK. It featured the Perkins A4.318 diesel engine and was in fact a close relative of the 180 built in the USA from 1965-74. The cab cladding was actually fitted by the distributors as the tractors were delivered with frame only as on the left.

The MF1100 was first seen in England at the 1967 Smithfield Show, and was powered by the Perkins 6.354 diesel engine. One of the larger models introduced in 1905 in the Western Hemisphere to suit Prairie farming its appeal on the UK market was aimed at the big farmer with a large arable acreage. The rear of the tractor is seen (opposite page bottom) whilst two overall views are shown on this page. It was produced until 1972. The 1130 which was not sold in the UK was the same tractor with a turbocharged engine.

Above: The 47HP 550 was the smallest of the 500 range initially offered in the United Kingdom. It used the Perkins A3.152 engine. The development of the 500 range was caused by the 'Q' cab legislation which came into effect from 1.9.77.

Below: Next in line was the 565 at 60HP with the Perkins A4.236 engine (derated). Whilst the cab with its modular design was intended to improve driver comfort, the lack of a right hand door did not endear the range to many operators. Dealers too were not too happy as the cab controls all had to be disconnected and the cab removed to effect certain rear end repairs.

Above and Below: The 575 offered 66HP and also used the Perkins A4.236 engine. The 500 series incorporated striking new styling and badging.

Above: The 595 was the largest of the 500 range offered in the United Kingdom and was not directly related to the other models in the 500 range as it had its ancestry in models produced in the Western Hemisphere.

Opposite page. The four wheel drive 1200 seen in the company of a Massey Harris 4WD dating from the late 1920s, and a selection of other models contemporary and historical.

The rear end of the 590. Showing the method of support for the cab.

Above left: The 230 was the smallest tractor in the 200 range and is seen here with rollbar and diesel engine.

Above right: The 245 with enhanced specification including rollbar and PAVT wheels. This tractor has a Continental Z145 petrol (gasoline) engine.

Below: The 240 seen in 'export' form without cab. This 34HP tractor was the 1970s equivalent of the TE-20. Production of 200 series tractors started at Banner Lane in 1979 with the 240, 265, 275 and 290 models.

Below: The 250 also used the Perkins AD3.152 engine governed to develop 40HP. This model and the smaller tractors in the range only offered an 8 speed transmission plus power assisted steering. Auxiliary hydraulics were only available on the 250, which was Banner Lane built from the end of 1982.

Below: The 270 featured a 55HP Perkins AD4.236 engine and the option of 12 speed Multi-Power. However auxiliary hydraulics were standard. The larger models also featured disk brakes built into the rear axle housings, actuated hydraulically. This model was also built at Banner Lane from the end of 1982.

*255 (above) and 265 models for the Canadian market
with rollbars.   Both models later used the Perkins
AD4.236 engine, that on the 255 being derated to give
only 52HP whilst the 265 gave 60HP. Some early 255
tractors were fitted with AD4.203 engines, and this
model was also available with a gasoline engine.*

*Opposite page bottom: The 285 along with the 1085;
details of the latter model can be found on page 49.*

Left: The 275 used the Perkins AD4.248 engine rated at 67HP and featured all the options available on the larger models.

Below: The 285 with its AD4.318 engine seen at work on a Canadian farm. This tractor incorporated 200 series rear transmission layout with 'straddle configuration' for the driver.

Below: The 290 was a 65HP tractor with Perkins AD.248 engine. Production of this model started at Banner Lane in 1979.

Below: The 78HP 298 began production at Coventry in 1984 but had been built in France since 1981. Note that this model has a frame support for the front axle.

Above: Safety legislation in the Western Hemisphere has always been somewhat behind that in Europe. The 1085 with its flat deck cab took account of both the increasing demand for cabs in the Western Hemisphere, and likely State legislation. It was sold from 1973-1979. Its ancestry was in the 1080, and with the 285 gave farmers in the USA a choice of two tractors of identical horsepower but with different driving positions. Safety considerations in the USA are mainly vested in each State, but the demand for tractors with cabs has increased steadily over the past twenty years or so.

In this look at MF up to the mid 1980s it has not been possible to cover every variation and specification produced. The complexities of building special models for certain territories and allocating special model numbers to them means that any future publication on Massey Ferguson will prove a very difficult one to write and produce.
It has also not been possible to provide complete serial number information due to difficulty in obtaining data on US and Canadian built tractors. The French numbering system is also rather complex; if this information does come to light in the future it will be made available either in the form of a supplementary insert or in our quarterly magazine "Vintage Tractor".

MASSEY FERGUSON MODEL DESIGNATIONS

TO-35	Detroit built tractor with Continental Z-134 engine, 1954-57. (5)
FE-40	Detroit built tractor with Continental Z-134 engine, 1956-57. (5) Ferguson
MH-50	Detroit built tractor with Continental Z-134 engine, 1955-58 (5) Massey.
FE-35	Standard built tractor with Standard engine 1956-58.
MF-35	Standard/ MF built tractor with Standard engine 1958-59
MF-35	MF built tractor with Perkins 3.152 engine 1959-62.
MF-35X	MF built tractor with Perkins A3-152 engine 1962-64.
MF-65	MF built tractor with Perkins 4.203 engine 1958-65.
MF-25	MF French built tractor with Perkins 4.107 engine 1963-65.
MF-88	MF Detriot built tractor with Continental Diesel 1960-1962.
MF Super 90.	MF Detriot built tractor with Perkins A4.300 engine 1961-1965.

100 Series.

MF-130	MF French built tractor with Perkins 4.107 engine, 1966-72
MF-135	MF built tractor with Perkins A3.152/ Continental Z145/ Perkins AG3.152 engine 1965-79.
MF-148	MF built tractor with Perkins A3.152 engine 1972-1979
MF-150	MF Detroit built tractor with engines as MF-135. 1965-75
MF-165	MF built tractor with Perkins AD4.203 engine 1965-71.
MF-168	MF built tractor with Perkins A4.212 engine 1971-1979.
MF-165	MF built tractor with Perkins A4.212 engine 1971-1979.
MF-175	MF built tractor with Perkins A4.236 engine 1965-1968
MF-180	MF Detriot built tractor with Perkins A4.236 engine 1965-74.
MF-178	MF built tractor with Perkins A4.248 engine 1968-1971
MF-185	MF built tractor with Perkins A4.248 engine 1971-1979
MF-188	MF built tractor with Perkins A4.248 engine 1971-1979
MF-1100	MF Detriot built tractor with Perkins A6.354 engine 1965-72.
MF-1130	MF Detriot built tractor with Perkins AT6.354 engine 1965-72

N.B. Most 100 series tractors sold in the Western Hemisphere were also available with gasoline engines. See engine specification table for details.

500 Series.

MF-550	MF built tractor with Perkins A3.152s engine
MF-565	MF built tractor with Perkins A4.236 engine
MF-575	MF built tractor with Perkins A4.236 engine
MF-590	MF built tractor with Perkins A4.248 engine

200 Series.

MF-230	MF Detroit built tractor with Perkins AD3.152 engine
MF-230	MF built tractor with Continental Z145 4 cylinder gasoline engine.
MF-240	MF built tractor with Perkins AD3.152 engine
MF-245	MF built tractor with Perkins AD3.152 engine
MF-245	MF built tractor with Continental Z145 4 cylinder gasoline engine.
MF-250	MF built tractor with Perkins AD3.152 engine
MF-255	MF built tractor with Perkins AD4.236 engine
MF-265	MF built tractor with Perkins AD4.236 engine
MF-270	MF built tractor with Perkins AD4.236 engine
MF-275	MF built tractor with Perkins AD4.248 engine
MF-285	MF built tractor with Perkins AD4.318 engine
MF-290	MF built tractor with Perkins AD4.248 engine
MF-298	MF built tractor with Perkins AD4.318.2 engine

N.B. The 200 series were originally built in the Western Hemisphere - production was then transferred to Banner Lane Coventry and the French MF plant.

Massey Ferguson Tractors
Engine Specifications

Make	Cyls	Bore x Stroke	CC.	Fuel HP	Used in.
Cont. Z-134	4	3.3125" x 3.875"	2195	G. 32.80	TO-35, F-40, (5)
Standard	4	80.96mm x101.6mm	2092	D. 26.00	TEF-20 (6)
Perkins P3(TA)	3	3.5" x 5"	2360	D. 34.00	Conversion pack.
Perkins P6(TA)	6	3.5" x 5"	4730	D. 46.00	MH744.
Perkins L4(TA)	4	4.25 x 4.75"	4420	D. 50.00	MH745
Standard	4	87mm x 92mm	2186	G. G/K 34.00	FE 35, 135 Petrol.
Standard 23C	4	84.14 x 101.6mm	2258	D. 34.00	FE35,
Perkins 4A-203	4	3.6" x 5".	3335	D. 55.50	MF65
Perkins 3.152	3	3.6" x 5".	2489	D. 35.00	MF35, MF50.
Perkins A3-152	3	3.6" x 5"	2500	D. 41.50	MF35X, MF50.
Perkins AD3-152	3	3.6 x 5"	2500*	D. 41.50	135, 230, 245, 240.
Perkins AD4-203	4	3.6 x 5"	3335	D. 55.50	65. 165.
Cont. G 176	4	3.58" x 4.38"	2883	G 46.92	65. (W.H.) 165
Cont. Z 145	4	3.375" x 4.062"	2376	G 35.36	135, 150, 230, 245.
Perkins AG3.152	3	3.6" x 5"	2489	G 35.00	Late 135/150.
Perkins AG4.212	4	3.875" x 4.5"	3472	G 55.00	165.
Perkins A4.212	4	3.875" x 4.5"	3472	D 58.30	late 165/168.
Perkins A4.236	4	3.875 x 5"	3865	D 63.34	175.
Perkins AD4.236	4	3.875 x 5"	3865	D 63.34	565, 575.
Perkins A4.248	4	3.980 x 5"	4062	D. 68.00	178.
Perkins AD4.248	4	3.980 x 5"	4062	D. 68.00	590.
Perkins A4.300	4	4.5" x 4.75"	4950	D. 68.00	Super 90.
Perkins A4.318	4	4.5" x 5"	5210	D 70.76	285, 298. 1085.
Cont. G 206	4	3.9" x 4.5"	3374	G. 62.33	175, 180
Perkins AG4.236	4	3.875" x 5"	3865	G. 62.00	175, 180
Perkins 4.107	4	3.125" x 3.5"	1752	D. 26.96	825, 130.
Perkins A6.354	6	3.875" x 5"	5798	D. 93.94	1100
Perkins AT6.354	6	3.875" x 5"	5798	D. 120.51	1130
Waukesha F320-G	6	4.125" x 4"	5341	G. 90.29	1100

Notes: G=Gasoline. G/K= Petrol/TVO. D=Diesel. TD=Turbocharged Diesel.
The numbers in brackets ( ) refer to the list of model codes below.

*Certain models had governor settings which limited the maximum engine speed to below the published ratings.

SERIAL NUMBERS

Unless indicated, the first serial number in each year is shown.

Ferguson 35/ Massey Ferguson 35 built at Coventry.

1956	1001	1961	220614
1957	9226	1962	267528
1958	79553	1963	307231
1959	125068	1964	352255
1960	171471	end	388382

First FE35 built October 1956.
First MF35 (Red/Grey) built November 1957
Last Standard 23c engine 166595.
First Perkins 3-152 engine 166596 (November 1959).
MF35X introduced December 1962 (with Multipower).

Massey Ferguson 65 Built at Coventry.

1958	500001	1962	551733
1959	510451	1963	552325
1960	520569	1964	593028
1961	533180	end	614024

First MF65 Mark I built December 1957.
First MF65 Mark II introduced November 1960
First A4-203 engine 531453.
Multipower Introduced August 1962.

Ferguson TO20/ TO30 Built by Harry Ferguson Inc. Detriot.

1948 (Oct)	1	1952	72680
1949	1808	1953	108645
1950	14660	1954	125959
1951	39163	end	140000

TO-30 cut in at Serial No. 60001 in August 1951.

Ferguson TO-35 Built by Massey Harris Ferguson Inc. Detroit.

1954	140001	1956	167157
1955	140006	1957	171741

TO-35 Gas Deluxe.

1958	178216	1960	203680
1959	188851	1961	207427

TO-35 Gas Special.

1958	183348	1960	203198
1959	185504	1961	209484

TO-35 Diesel

1958	180742	1960	203360
1959	187719	1961	203680

Massey Ferguson MF-35 Built by Massey Ferguson Inc. Detroit.

1960	204181	1962	222207
1961	211071	1963	235123.PA

Ferguson 40 Built by Massey Harris Ferguson Inc. Detroit.

1956	400001	1957	405671

Massey Harris 50 Built by Massey Harris Ferguson Inc. Detroit.

1955	500001	1957	510764
1956	500473	1958	515708

Following the cessation of the two line policy (F-40 and MH-50 tractors were assembled on the same production line), the model became the MF-50.

Massey Ferguson 50 Built by Massey Ferguson Inc. Detroit.

1959	522693	1962	529821
1960	528163	1963	533422
1961	528418	1964	536062

Massey Ferguson 65 Built by Massey Ferguson Inc. Detroit.

1958	650001	1962	685370
1959	661164	1963	693040
1960	671379	1964	701057
1961	680210		

Massey Ferguson 85 Built by Massey Ferguson Inc.

1959	800001	1961	807750
1960	804355	1962	808564

Massey Ferguson 88 Built by Massey Ferguson Inc.

1959	880001	1961	807750
1960	881453	1962	808564

Massey Ferguson 90 Built by Massey Ferguson Inc.

1962	810000	1964	816113
1963	813170	1965	819342

Massey Ferguson 90WR Built by Massey Ferguson Inc.

1962	885000	1963	886829
1963	885870	1964	888238

100 Series. Banner Lane Coventry Build. Massey Ferguson 135.

1965	101	1969	117429
1966	30283	1970	141426
1967	67597	1971	162200
1968	93305		

Massey Ferguson 135 updated.

1971	400001	1976	457866

1972	403518	1977	469335
1973	419583	1978	479192
1974	432709	1979	487350
1975	445602	end	490714

Massey Ferguson 165.

1965	500001	1969	563701
1966	512207	1970	581457
1967	530825	1971	597745
1968	547384		

Massey Ferguson 165 updated.

1971	100001	1976	145432
1972	103622	1977	155687
1973	116353	1978	164417
1974	126448	1979	173144
1975	135036	end	173696

Massey Ferguson 175 (178 from 1968)

1965	700001	1969	732158
1966	705652	1970	740301
1967	714166	1971	747283
1968	722679	1972	753108

Massey Ferguson 175 S

1968	650000	1971	656011
1969	652061	1972	657362
1970	653721		

Massey Ferguson 148

1972	600001	1977	609159
1973	602153	1978	609969
1974	604449	1979	610893
1975	605578	end	610982
1976	607701		

Massey Ferguson 168

1971	250001	1976	258064
1972	250005	1977	259959
1973	252121	1978	260617
1974	254307	1979	261103
1975	255967	end	261173

Massey Ferguson 185

1971	300001	1976	326109
1972	302833	1977	332107
1973	310398	1978	335211
1974	315219	1979	339755
1975	319923	end	340096

Massey Ferguson 188

1971	350001	1976	365087
1972	350006	1977	368350
1973	353296	1978	370156
1974	357063	1979	371306
1975	360784	end	371333

100 Series.   Built in USA. 1964-1966.

Massey Ferguson 135

1964	641000001
1965	641001909
1966	641014871

Massey Ferguson 150

1964	642000001
1965	642000015
1966	631000505

Massey Ferguson 165

1964	643000001
1965	643000003
1966	643000149

Massey Ferguson 175

1964	644000001
1965	644000004
1966	644000214

Massey Ferguson 180

1964	645000001
1965	645000002
1966	647000047

100 Series built in USA 1967-1969.
A common series was used for 150/165/175 and 180 tractors.

1967	9A10001
1968	9A39836
1969	9A63158

1000 Series built 1964-1966.

Massey Ferguson 1100

1964	650000001
1965	650000003
1966	650000831

Massey Ferguson 1130

1964	650500001
1965	650500004
1966	651500049

1000 Series built 1967-1969.
A common series was used for 1100/1130 and 1080 tractors.

1967	9B10001
1968	9B14693
1969	9B18673.

200 Series, Banner Lane Coventry Build.

Massey Ferguson 240

| 1979 | 500001 | 1981 | 512212 |
| 1980 | 505157 | 1982 | 518907* |

Massey Ferguson 265

| 1979 | 175001 | 1981 | 185205 |
| 1980 | 178332 | 1982 | 190605* |

Massey Ferguson 275 (Not sold in UK)

| 1979 | 210001 | 1981 | 212632 |
| 1980 | 210959 | 1982 | 220683 |

Massey Ferguson 290

1979	341001	1981	371428
1980	342988	1982	383320
to	347000		
1980	371334		
to	371427		

500 Series Banner Lane Coventry build.

Massey Ferguson 550

1976	615001	1980	619911
1977	615193	1981	620531
1978	616891	1982	620722
1979	619008	to	620767 end.

Massey Ferguson 565

1976	650001	1980	657826
1977	651188	1981	658852
1978	653459	1982	659159
1979	656575	to	659189 end.

Massey Ferguson 575

1976	265001	1980	270028
1977	265982	1981	271271
1978	267645	1982	271595
1979	269282	to	271630 end.

Massey Ferguson 590

1976	375001	1980	379928
1977	375914	1981	381382
1978	377188	1982	382238
1979	379077	to	382396 end.

Massey Ferguson 1200

1974	900001	1978	901508
1975	900229	1979	901845
1976	900748	to	902059 end.
1977	901021		

Below: A celebration was held to mark the 21st Anniversary of tractor production at Banner Lane. Alex Patterson, Jimmy Jones, and John Beith pose with Ferguson TE-20 number one.

Above: We can now reveal the identity of the bottom picture on page 25. Following the MF/EBRO agreement in 1966 there appeared some 'bastard' models starting with the EBRO 155, which featured MF 100 series tinwork but underneath was really a Spanish built Fordson Super Major. When Ebro set its sights on the export market in the early seventies the 155 was restyled to give it a 'non MF' appearance and finished in Blue and Silver. Note also the restyled fenders and front axle.

Centre: By fitting a Perkins 4.236 engine giving 71BHP @ 2100 RPM, to the basic unit the Ebro 470 produced a further hybrid which was built until the mid 1980s.

Bottom: With a 6.305 engine installed giving 82BHP @ 2100RPM, you had the Ebro 684E, still with the faithful Fordson Major transmission.

Above: The IMT 539 is instantly recognisable as the MF35.
Industrija Masina Traktora of Beograd built this tractor under licence.   Readers will note that a six speed gearbox was provided - "Multi-Power" was not licensed to IMT!

Below: Less recognisable but of similar ancestry is the IMT 542. Whilst this model also used the Perkins A3.152 engine, certain aspects of the transmission differed from MF standards, as a gearbox which provided 10 forward and 2 reverse gears was fitted, and this provided for four operating gears with synchromesh